YOU ARE SWEET AS YOU ARE

COPYRIGHT © 2024 BY CAITLYN JAGGER
ALL RIGHTS RESERVED. NO PART OF THIS PUBLICATION MAY BE REPRODUCED, DISTRIBUTED, OR TRANSMITTED IN ANY FORM OR BY ANY MEANS, INCLUDING PHOTOCOPYING, RECORDING, OR OTHER ELECTRONIC OR MECHANICAL METHODS, WITHOUT THE PRIOR WRITTEN PERMISSION OF THE PUBLISHER, EXCEPT IN THE CASE OF BRIEF QUOTATIONS EMBODIED IN CRITICAL REVIEWS AND CERTAIN OTHER NONCOMMERCIAL USES PERMITTED BY COPYRIGHT LAW.

DESIGN © 2024 BY CAITLYN JAGGER
PUBLISHED BY CAITLYN JAGGER BOOKS
ISBN: 978-1-0670232-5-6

FOR INFORMATION REGARDING PERMISSION, WRITE TO INFO@CAITLYNJAGGERBOOKS.COM, ATTENTION: PERMISSIONS.
HOW MANY SUGARS IS A WORK OF FICTION. NAMES, CHARACTERS, PLACES, AND INCIDENTS EITHER ARE THE PRODUCT OF THE AUTHOR'S IMAGINATION OR ARE USED FICTITIOUSLY. ANY RESEMBLANCE TO ACTUAL PERSONS, LIVING OR DEAD, EVENTS, OR LOCALES IS ENTIRELY COINCIDENTAL.
DESIGN BY CAITLYN JAGGER

VISIT WWW.CAITLYNJAGGERBOOKS.COM FOR INFORMATION ON OTHER TITLES.
NATIONAL LIBRARY OF NEW ZEALAND CATALOGUING-IN-PUBLICATION DATA:
JAGGER, CAITLYN. HOW MANY SUGARS / CAITLYN JAGGER; WRITTEN & DESIGNED BY CAITLYN JAGGER. – FIRST EDITION.

ENOUGH!

SAID THE LEAF TO THE COFFEE BEAN.

I DON'T NEED EXTRA SWEETNESS IN MY CUP!

AND I DON'T NEED TO TELL YOU WHAT MAKES ME UP!

NO BITTERNESS IN MY WELL CARED FOR LEAVES,

I'M SWEET AS I AM, AND THAT'S ALL I NEED.

I HAVE MANY DIFFERENT VARIETIES,

ALL FULL OF FLAVOUR,

AND EACH IS AS NICE,
DEPENDING ON YOUR NATURE.

I CAN BE RELAXING, I CAN BE CALMING, I CAN BE **INVIGORATING OR SOOTHING.**

I CAN BE ANYTHING I WANT,
AND THAT'S MINE FOR CHOOSING!

IF YOU ONLY WANT ME TO BE AS YOU ARE,

I WILL NEVER COMPARE,

AS WE ARE DIFFERENT – BY FAR!

COFFEE,
YOU ARE A GIFT
TO THOSE WHO LIKE YOUR PEP,

BUT I WILL COME AS I AM,
AND BE THERE FOR THE REST!

I HAVE MANY DIFFERENT VARIETIES
AND ALL ARE SUPERB!

THE QUESTION IS SILLY – ENJOY ME NATURALLY!

Discover our other collections:
Our Mother, Earth

A collection of stories focused on the importance of self-sustainability, told through Bean and her wonderful group of eco-friendly pals!

Visit www.caitlynjaggerbooks.com to find out more!

Discover our other collections:
Ocean Adventures

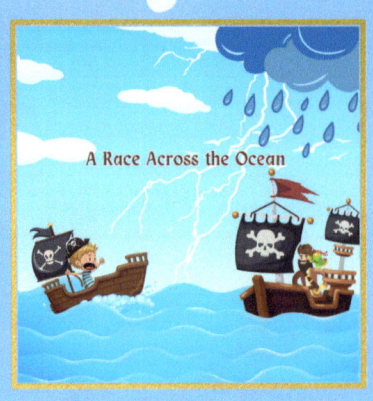  

A series of tales on the Seven Seas, featuring Captain Jack and all his fishy friends! Discover the full collection to learn lessons on the importance of friendship, perseverance and knowing when to ask for help.

Visit www.caitlynjaggerbooks.com to find out more!